Camille Chronicles

∽

Jennifer Lagier

FUTURECYCLE PRESS
www.futurecycle.org

Cover artwork by Gene McCormick; author photo by herself; cover and interior design by Diane Kistner; Cambria text with Crete Round titling

Library of Congress Control Number: 2021946193

Published by FutureCycle Press
Athens, Georgia, USA

ISBN 978-1-952593-31-4

Dedicated to Joan Colby

Contents

Camille Vérité

Camille Abroad

Camille Morphs to Crone

Camille Mobilizes

Camille Comes Unglued

*"Sweetie, if you're not living on the edge,
then you're taking up space."*
—Florynce Kennedy

Camille Vérité

∾

"No woman gets an orgasm from shining the kitchen floor."
—Betty Friedan

On the Town

The barista at Fermentations
shows Camille sixteen stitches
over her eyebrow, explains
how the local physician's assistant
sewed her up for only $35.
She promises an introduction,
Camille's insurance against
future tanked-up disasters;
says when she moves here,
they'll be best buds forever.
At Mozzi's, old drunken hippies
play rotation pool.
Nailed to the ceiling,
a wagon wheel light,
signs from bankrupt local businesses.
Over-the-hill sluts shriek,
expose more side boob
than necessary,
take up all the bar stools.
A bright yellow poster
hangs on the door:
Guys: No Shirt, No Service
Gals: No Shirt, Free Drinks
Camille sighs, thinks:
This is my kingdom;
these are my people.

Art of the Wild

Camille purrs and arches her back.
The artist, who is also her lover, paints a forest:
jungle green circles around swollen breasts.
With one finger, he daubs orange over each nipple,
sensual bullseyes that harden, welcome his touch.

As she stretches cat-like across his sofa,
he transforms her into a reclining zebra,
streaks her rib cage black and white.
Her thighs open like bright blue butterflies,
reveal the shocking pink secret inside.

Camille Behind the Wheel

She slips into a leather halter top
pair of cutoffs, strappy stilettos.
Slides into her Jaguar convertible,
ready to travel, hit the road
for today's Big Sur adventure,
"Going to California" at high decibel
her choice of soundtrack.
Accelerates down Highway One
toward Nepenthe for blinis,
a juicy Ambrosia burger.
Tailgates pokey tourists.
Flips off an obnoxious trucker.
Streaky hair tousled by wind,
her mascaraed cat eyes hide
behind Versace glasses.
Camille is hungry and on the prowl
for a bohemian afternoon
with a throwaway lover.

Camille and the Criminal Element

Bad boys seduce her.
Tattooed teenage criminals
expelled for boozing or doping.
The ones in detention who never
bothered with academics or sports.

These are the guys
who make her feel wicked,
inhabit hot dreams,
teach her how to sneak
out the window at night.

Sullen strays who take
what they want without
any sense of loyalty or obligation,
shun collars and leashes,
feed on what they take down.

Hoot and Holler

At the Running Iron, Camille struts her stuff,
demonstrates cowboy culture on the skids,
clogs, slides and twirls to a shit-kicker band.

It's Hoot and Holler night. Eagerly, she
encourages a barmaid with a pair of water pistols
to shoot lime juice, then tequila, into her mouth.

After more than a few, she's star of the bar,
ready to mosey down the street to Miss Lila's,
finally get that winking mermaid tattoo.

Camille Vérité

She sits at the bar, scans her surroundings,
scents a few single men.
Ignoring the young and obvious,
she chooses a secretive lover, incognito,
checking him out from the shadows.
Every player understands the rules:
previous and existing claims are void.
She wants him, obsesses.
Tilting her head, she sweeps streaked hair
behind an ear, offers submission.
He approaches; she provides a gambit,
licks the martini glass rim.
Silently, he claims what he knows he owns,
presses his lips, hard, against her neck.
Teeth nibble soft flesh.

Exercise in Restraint

Camille sees him
stretched out on his back
against a thin rubber
exercise mat like
a luscious entrée.
His tee shirt
rides up, reveals
dark body hair against
a pale, vulnerable belly,
a provocative trail that
travels south
to warmer regions
that tempt and intrigue.
As he performs slow,
sinuous crunches,
she is mesmerized
by what bulges
against baggy shorts.
Breathless, she imagines
straddling his hips,
riding him to
the finish line.
She is a sucker
for hardness.

Next Ex-Husband Interviews

Camille hands out maps and smiles
at the Concours d'Elegance
in Pebble Beach.
She has stationed herself
between two Rolls Royces
near the Porsche Pavilion
where the richer boys roam.

Older trophy wives,
now gone to menopause,
glare as she flirts with their men.
Camille could have her pick
of international millionaires,
celebrity movie stars, local players.
As they examine each sleek, classic model,
she adjusts her tight tee shirt, licks her wet lips.

Peaches and Camille, Post Pinot Noir

Still tipsy from two glasses of wine and an Irish coffee,
she returns to the room, strips off her clothes, pulls on
a tight animal-print swimsuit, heads out the door.

When she wades, then slides, into the roiling hot tub,
children and their parents scatter. Out of the darkness
comes the red bikinied woman she earlier met at the bar.

Side by side, the women allow their bare legs to drift
and flutter, soft shoulders coming closer, then touching.
They talk, share a bit more. One is blonde, the other brunette.

Later they meander up a single staircase, giggle
at the resumption of unending rainfall, marvel at how
the alcohol has left them with no inhibitions at all.

Camille at the Creekside Café

The bill of fare is
what Camille considers
culinary foreplay.
She lets Ramon's recitation
of daily specials
tempt and arouse her.
Appetite piqued,
she savors his grin,
the undivided attention.
Asks for something
satisfying and hot,
not necessarily a dish
on the regular menu.
Camille can tell he is eager
to please, that he
will efficiently serve her.
Purrs over the salsa.
Praises his signature
breakfast burrito.
Eats every bite.
Knocks back a mimosa.
Is a generous tipper.

I See Rumps

Camille performs
downward-facing dog
at the "Just for You"
yoga class,
tries to concentrate,
chokes back a laugh.
Around her,
lumpy men in sweats,
chunky women
in straining spandex,
asses high in the air.
She feels gravity
as it pulls
breasts and belly.
Knows she is
limber but vulnerable,
tush aimed
at the ceiling.
Feels a surging
hot flash as the
hunky instructor's
hands grip her hipbones.

Teaser

Camille contemplates
the gardener:
tight ass,
intriguing jeans-bulge,
six-pack abdomen,
muscular biceps.
Thinks of D. H. Lawrence,
his sensual women—
Connie Chatterley
with the gamekeeper,
a satisfying yet
unsuitable lover.
Rafael grins,
white teeth against
cappuccino tan.
She fantasizes him lightly
nibbling her nipples,
rough hands moving
against pale, silky skin.
Open thighs ache;
her back arches,
toes curl.
She quivers, feels him
push deep inside her.

Like a Leper in a Beauty Contest

Camille pumps iron
at the Wellness Center
three times a week.
Wears headphones
to extinguish
Fox News commentators,
Rush Limbaugh,
Bill O'Reilly,
red-faced and yelling
from all four TVs.
Cranks up "Dark Side of the Moon"
when the muscular
paramilitary guy
with racist tattoos
occupies a
nearby lifecycle.
He demands attention
as he rants,
recites lists
of who should
be exterminated,
deported or jailed.
Then invites her
out for a drink.
By the end
of her workout,
she is exhausted,
worn out from
the effort of
biting her tongue.

Looking for Mr. Goodtime

After midnight in a Barbary Coast bar,
Camille sees herself reflected between tiers
of vodka bottles, whiskey, tequila.
A biker in black leather
bumps her stool, creating weird vibes.
His history is inked on brawny arms,
a still-oozing wound on the side of his head.
Camille's own roadmap is less visible,
but he intuits the general itinerary,
slides beside her, orders Jack Daniels neat.
Hey babe, he drawls, *you look like a girl
who could use some company.*
With one finger, he traces spider-web scars
crisscrossing the underside of her wrists.
They are castaways, seek the same alcoholic oasis,
another inevitable car-crash affair.
Now his hand caresses her thigh.
He pulls her closer, signals the bartender.
Honey, let me buy you a drink.

Kryptonite

Camille contemplates her boy toy
as he sucks medical-grade marijuana
from a brand new inhaler.
Later, he nods off, snores,
spills warm beer on her sofa.

This is not what she had in mind
when she took a young lover.
She notices overexposure
has diminished his luster.
Samson, now shorn, sleeps till noon,
anesthetized by vodka and oxycodone.

Superman has reverted to
a forgettable Clark Kent who
prefers being in a coma to employment.
Camille misses her man of steel,
the one capable of leaping tall buildings,
stopping locomotives, quenching her fire.

Put Out Water With Fire

Camille is pissed,
has promised
herself there would be
no more boyfriends, lovers,
especially not husbands.
Now she is hooked,
has it bad
for the newest
delinquent who
disrupts nights,
short-circuits writing,
hardens her nipples.
One more pseudo
Jack Kerouac,
Hank Chinaski,
or e. e. cummings.
Camille hates her weakness,
already knows
disappointment,
betrayal, and major
heartbreak
are coming.

Camille Abroad

∞

"Good girls go to heaven, bad girls go everywhere."
—*Unknown*

So Long As It Comes Easy

Ah, the irony,
Camille reflects.
Her first week
of estrogen cream
and her partner
announces he's lost
any sex drive.
What's a girl to do?
she wonders.
Considers computer dating,
casual hookups.
Discovers the
Good Vibrations website.
Studies a column titled,
"Kink for Beginners."
Researches toys to give
herself pleasure.
The Rabbit Pearl
(originally seen
on *Sex and the City*)
advertises pure bliss
for only $65.
She browses
for a new lover
among the
bestsellers.

Same Old Movie

Camille has been down this road before.
Recognizes all the red flags.
He is distant, cool.
Lost his appetite.
Hasn't wanted sex in months.
Talks less and less.
Works all night at the office.
Won't answer emails or phone.
Says it's nothing personal.
Just going through a phase.
Wants to be by himself.
Camille is out of patience,
sick of the same old routine.
She imagines cutting her losses.
Frosting her hair, packing a bag.
Climbing on a plane.
She'd welcome new scenery,
a fresh start in a warm, foreign land,
meeting no end of fascinating,
sensual, intellectual men.

Rerun

Camille has a ringside seat
at the end of the bar
in the No Mercy Saloon.
From here, she can watch
over-the-hill players as they ply
desperate divorcées in their forties
and twentysomething airheads
with umbrella drinks.

She has played a starring role
in similar romantic farces.
Decides to sit this one out,
relax and observe.
Can mime common pick-up lines
and flirty responses.

Sees an older man on the
opposite side of the counter.
He, too, is taking a breather,
enjoying the drama.
He catches her eye, tips his glass,
smiles in amusement.

She feels something stir,
knocks back the last of her wine.
Camille already knows how it ends
but figures "what the hell...."
Accepts his kind offer of refill.

Expatriate

Camille breezes through security,
unpacks her laptop, checks email,
Facebook from an airport café.
The trim waiter brings hot chowder,
an icy mimosa, offers tempting desserts.

In an hour, she'll lift off from San Francisco,
wave goodbye to parched California:
crowded cookie-cutter houses,
empty reservoirs,
snowless Sierras.

At the boarding gate,
she unclenches,
imagines a clean slate,
reinvented reality,
herself starting over.

Departure from Been-there-and-done-it-to-death.
Destination: Adventure. Possibility. Barcelona. Madrid.

Alicante

Camille wanders wonderland byways:
dizzying Paseo de la Explanada de España,
secret plazas, their kiosks and fountains,
skinny alleys decorated with fantastical mushrooms.

She discovers tiny cafés serving pizza and tapas.
Treats herself to Spanish beer, then flan
complimented by cups of espresso.
Returns the smile of a dark Spaniard who winks,
generously foots the bill for her sangria.

Watches beautiful men holding hands,
sipping champagne at a yacht harbor bistro.
Spends the night in a penthouse overlooking
high-rise apartments, twitching ocean,
flickering streetlights.

From between black satin sheets,
she imagines Dos Passos, Hemingway, Stein;
dreams of matadors, bullfights,
an Iberian world filled with fiery lovers.

Carne

While in Spain, Camille renounces
her vegetarian past, craves meat
in every form, morning and night.
Salivates over salami, thin prosciutto slices,
grows wet at the sight of foil-wrapped ham.

Crisp bacon tempts,
weans her from breakfast yogurt.
Siren song of steak and sangria for lunch.
By dinner, her appetite is reduced
to bruschetta sprinkled with chorizo,
a bit of green salad, shards of hard cheese.

All night she fantasizes flesh in many forms:
succulent pork, mouth-watering beef.
Sleeps soundly, lost in carnal dreams.

Madrid

Policía in blue uniforms twirling black mausers
form a mandatory reception line leading into the train
    terminal.
Camille is divested of purse and belt, subjected to a full-body
    scan.

In the coach car, passengers sit, two by two.
An attendant pushes a squeaky cart down the narrow aisle,
dispenses espresso, newspapers, travel advice.

Green fields, leafless vineyards, graffiti flash by.
A gravel-voiced matron shouts *¡Hola!*
conversing at high decibel on her oversized phone.

Civil guardsmen on every corner recall bloody terrorist
    bombings.
Mimes and street performers command crammed Madrid
    plazas,
banter with tourists, beg for coins and applause.

At the Prada, cathedrals, museums, more soldiers swarm.
Camille finds a peaceful table under pink-blossoming trees.
Sips wine in a tiny demilitarized zone.

Mimo

Camille has known her share of changelings.
This silver Spaniard with metallic stage props
is simply one more performance artist
camouflaged by imaginative makeup.
He postures, plays to the crowd,
donation can before his podium,
aggressively shilling for money.

The man has neither humility nor shame.
Stares and smirks, intuits exactly
what Camille is thinking
as she flings a small coin,
pauses to appraise
his trim, wiry physique.

Camille is ready
to reinvent her persona.
Vows to diet, try lipo,
inject Botox, some filler.
Emulate a chameleon,
craft a new body and face.

Plaza Major

It's barely 11 a.m., and the plaza is crowded.
Camille wanders among hustlers,
acrobats, mimes, *policía* in blue uniforms
who cradle black rifles.

Pale heroin addicts sprawl against sunlit walls.
Outside cafés, every table is crowded.
Harried waitresses carry baskets of bread,
Spanish omelets, cups of fragrant espresso.

A bridal party spills from a nearby chapel,
so immature they look like children in costumes.
Camille has explored this option,
has no desire for tradition or husbands.

She is still discovering who she is,
what she can achieve; wants to learn
other languages, savor
alternative continents, cultures.

Negra y Ángel

A dark Iberian angel leads Camille
past her comfort zone
through a canyon of vintage apartments,
along cracked, slanting sidewalks,
on her way to antique city center,
then to the sea.

Around her, spray-painted gang slogans,
intricate graffiti artwork.
Children wave paper streamers on sticks.
Elderly men and women pull shopping carts
or hold leashes tethered to small, ratty dogs.

Outside each *tienda,*
black-stockinged shop girls cluster,
clutching lit cigarettes;
gesture and share juicy gossip;
blow blue smoke into the brisk breeze,
howl with laughter.

Beach Esplanade

Camille explores the old town beach promenade.
Dizzying bands of cream, green and rust tiles wriggle
between inns, marketplace booths, white swaths of sand.
Before 10 a.m., a thin stream of curious tourists.
Here and there, an elderly couple walking their dog.

She marvels at pastel high-rise apartments—
their wrought iron balconies floating gardens
of scarlet geranium, vivid nasturtium—
imagines what it must look like at night,
boisterous crowds traversing patterned path,
waving ever-present cigarettes, clutching cold beers.

From her café table abutting the esplanade,
she sips potent espresso, watches joggers,
a shirtless rollerblader with muscular legs,
and sighs at the sight of his rippling abs.

Procesión

At Plaza de Santa Maria, Camille discovers
a colorful, noisy parade.
Women blow bagpipes, click castanets.
Vested men wave lettered banners,
strum their wooden guitars.

Tourists and shoppers merge
with exuberant musicians and marchers.
Diners spill onto sidewalks
from dim, cave-like cafés.

Camille leans against a lamppost,
nods to a passing cleric
who glares, gives her the once-over,
makes the evil eye sign.

One vivacious gent pauses, winks,
mimes holding a wine glass.
They rendezvous in a nearby bistro
where she welcomes seduction,
wakes to luminous sunrise.

Tapas y Tequila

After stumbling into the midst of a church procession,
Camille, who is allergic to piety, craves an antidote to religion.
Heads to Plaza Santa Barbara and her favorite café.
Orders tapas and tequila, discreetly settles into a nook,
eavesdrops on couples canoodling at dark corner tables.

Bartender Luis knows her weaknesses, serves local scandal
in lisping Spanish over espresso, sangria.
Chalks today's paella specials on blackboards
hung from ancient stone walls at the foot of a staircase.
Croons sexily with music videos, holds out a hand,
invites her to join him.

When in Spain, she thinks, knocking back a shot,
then grinds her way to the dance floor.

Emigrada

Camille considers renouncing American citizenship,
relocating to a funky Alicante flat
overlooking cafés and pocket parks,
a glimpse of silvery ocean.

She imagines morning excursions
tethered to the leash of a fat, spoiled Chihuahua,
casual flirtations with lively gentlemen
still in possession of that certain sparkle.

Hers would be the wrought iron balcony
spilling red geraniums, after-dark laughter.
She envisions intimacy on her terrace, sipping wine
beside the evening's hot lover.

Rainstorm

As Camille dejectedly packs her suitcase,
the Alicante skies open, wash ancient buildings
and congested streets with silver downpour.
Thunder grumbles, wallops rain from storm clouds,
matches her conflicting emotions, dark mood.

The last day in Spain, and there are still
so many unexplored cantinas;
but her return flight to California
will lift off just after dawn.

Pink trees shower wet streets
with wind-propelled blossoms.
She digs out her passport, breaks down her computer.

Tomorrow, she'll clear customs in Madrid,
then again in Chicago; suffer reentry jet lag;
sleep overnight, if she can, in San Francisco.

Camille reviews names in her phone book,
friends with whom to share a glass of wine
and exaggerated stories of lewd adventures.

Camille Morphs to Crone

֍

"A crone is a woman who has found her voice."
—*Jean Shinoda Bolen*

Mane Events

A chubby toddler,
Camille possessed a few golden wisps.
When the 1950's pixie cut grew out,
her mother wove thin hair
into tight, skinny braids.
By the early 60s, she wore
bleached, feathered highlights
over a ratted beehive
to accompany poodle skirts, fluffy slips.
During the Summer of Love,
Camille smoked dope, visited Haight-Ashbury
clad in Nehru jacket,
flat, ironed locks and leather headband,
paisley bell-bottomed pants.
The 70s brought women's lib
and a messy divorce.
She flaunted a blonde Afro
 braless beneath skimpy tank tops,
wore peg-legged tiny jeans.
During late 80s, early 90s,
she traded classic pageboy
for moussed punk spikes,
message tee shirts,
anti-war picket signs.
Now Camille wrestles faded cowlicks,
refuses to consider blue tresses, phony wig,
pays a professional to paint auburn streaks
through her anemic mane,
resurrect vanished youth.

Loud Laughing Wenches

Young wenches at Doc Ricketts'
crowd the bar, cadge free drinks
from horny tourists out slumming.
Display their long legs,
hot pink toenails,
uplifted cleavage.

Camille wallows in sangria,
cynicism and Amy Winehouse.
Until tonight, didn't realize
she'd exceeded her expiry date.
Regrets unconsummated lust
she has squandered.
Contemplates a sexless tomorrow.

Camille remembers taut, carefree youth,
turning heads, fending off passes.
Surveys the sorry lot of sodden men
spilling beer and complaining.
Sighs, buys her own glass of wine.
Will take herself home for a night
of old schmaltzy movies.

Moving Toward Death

Camille recognizes the slow dance
toward undignified mortality.
Despises drooping breasts,
multiplying wrinkles,
slight incontinence
when she laughs or sneezes.

Laments thinning hair,
proliferation of age spots.
Wonders how long
before sex drive evaporates,
mobility shrinks,
short-term memory vanishes.

Refuses to relinquish
sardonic personality,
caustic opinions,
hard-won independence.

Seeks disillusioned rebels
with an affinity for
weed, wine and irreverence
to join her crone revolution.

Shot to Hell

It's like putting lipstick on a pig,
Camille thinks, painting cracked toenails.
Her hand shakes, smears scarlet
onto dry skin where it doesn't belong.
She has trouble bending—a growing
fat roll circling her belly gets in the way.
She'd laugh, but that would cause her
to pee, despite thousands of kegels.

At the mirror, she beholds a blurry image
that looks like a younger version
of her elderly mother.
Leans in to pluck chin hairs,
count the new wrinkles.
Sighs as she remembers
clutching a man between thighs
now veined and flabby.
Misses seduction on cool sheets
during sultry Mediterranean summers.

No Way Out

Camille spies an old lover
sitting across the room
in her favorite café.
He huddles in a corner,
scowls at the menu,
seems dejected, fatigued.

She remembers drunken Fridays,
fondling one another, sharing shots
in discreet, sleazy bars.
Stoned lust followed by hours
of sexual capers.

Now a gold band strangles his finger.
She imagines him in bed by nine,
swaddled in geezer pajamas,
banished to his side
of chaste marital mattress.

Allergic to commitment,
she misses his hands, camaraderie.
She wonders why she aches.

Camille Morphs to Crone

Watch her balloon
before your eyes.
Slender ribs disappear
under pasty flab.
Her sexy growl
sounds more like
deep smoker's rasp.
Goddess breasts deflate,
unused, untouched,
nipples no longer perky.
Juicy nights, discontinued,
are fairy tales from the past.
Bikini wax is unnecessary,
not worth the trouble.
Everything down there
is in deep hibernation.
Time hasn't been kind.
She wakes late,
arthritic and cranky,
with leg stubble
and more wrinkles,
overpowered
by her own
morning breath.

So Much Has Gone

Camille contemplates a gray pubic hair.,
critiques her naked self in the full-length mirror:
belly and breasts beginning to sag,
silver laparoscopy scars,
what was once golden and taut
now drooping, wrinkled or flat.

It's confusing—she feels nineteen inside.
Her nipples still stand at attention,
face flushes, juices flow
when aroused by a man.

She knows who she is,
what she wants out of life.
Then, just as she hits her peak,
this goddamned body
develops a mind of its own,
starts falling apart.

Sliced Like Pie

Camille now has separate doctors
for each body part, disease, mental dysfunction.
Divides her life between free-spirit bohemian,
recovering lover, responsible daughter.
Is energetic in early morning:
power-walks miles of trail,
invites her poetry muse
to join her for coffee.
By mid-afternoon, she begins to sag,
craves a long, quiet nap
with two sleepy dogs
on a comfortable sofa.
Becomes what she has always feared:
a difficult, middle-aged woman.
Transforms from sexy, lively dynamo
into cranky shrew.

Sadly Sane

Camille is sick
of being sensible,
paying bills,
dumping trash,
buying groceries,
cooking dinner,
doing laundry.

She wants to resurrect
her old inner hippie,
turn on, tune in, drop out.
Less work and more play.
Poetry, music, meditation,
being naked in nature.

Adulthood isn't
what she had expected,
freedom cancelled
by unending projects.
She pines for playmates
to inspire delinquency,
join her rebellion.

Don't Lament Lost Youth

Camille dons a fuchsia smock,
reclines in a leather chair
as the nurse scrubs alcohol
into her face, explains procedures.

First, Botox injected here and there
to remove forehead furrows,
a jab at the end of each brow
to lift sagging eyelids.

Next, topical anesthetic,
then Novocain shots,
thin lips rejuvenated
by syringes loaded with filler.

The specialist inserts a needle,
lifts raw flesh to encourage
growth of new collagen
under each wrinkle.

Camille emerges with pouty mouth,
no marionette creases—
but she'll need ice packs and arnica
to minimize swelling and bruising.

Eventually, she'll invest
in coolsculpting treatments
to freeze away stubborn fat,
restore taut chin, neck and belly.

Camille endures pain
to emulate youth.
Spends a fortune to purchase
fleeting Frankenstein beauty.

AARP Booty Call

Camille meets Roy at Applebee's
for an Early Bird Dinner.
They connected online at SeniorPeople.com,
found each other's profile intriguing.
Enjoyed the "before" and "after" photos,
the battle wounds of aging.

Both still have their own teeth,
a sense of humor,
raging libidos.
Qualify for AARP discounts
at restaurants, motels.
Love to eat, drink and travel.

After more dates,
they share a bed, discover
they can laugh at arthritic hips,
stretch marks, sagging boobs,
Cialis and wrinkles.

All that's missing
is flexibility, stamina—
nothing yoga can't cure.

Once You Get the Taste

Camille is sick
of hearing excuses.
Is fed up with pharmacists
who won't answer their phone
or communicate with her doctor.
Can't bear the thought
of one more blood test,
mammogram, x-ray.
Is convinced pinot noir
is a better mood stabilizer
than Zoloft, Lexapro, Prozac.
Has decided to stop
holding her tongue,
being polite,
putting up with alarmist
endocrinologist bullshit.
Rejects civility
when confronted
with condescending physicians.
Doesn't care
if she is rude,
disruptive,
hurts some incompetent
phlebotomist's feelings.
Swears off traditional medicine.
Turns to exercise, natural remedies.
Avoids laboratories, specialists,
outpatient clinics.

Can't Hear

Camille complains about
her mumbling lover.
Swears the TV is turned too low.
Is frustrated when friends reveal
juicy secrets she can't decipher,
blames noisy restaurants.

Irritated, she submits
to an audiologist's testing.
Is pissed to discover
a profound hearing loss
that can't be explained.

On the bright side,
she considers Fox News blaring
from every gym monitor,
offensive asides in the weight room,
the benefits of deafness when surrounded
by loud, low-IQ men.

This Tired Machine

Camille swears the aging laptop,
sporadically functional Fitbit,
have declared a fatwa against her.
They sabotage writing and exercise,
life-saving mental health outlets.

At night, garden twinkle lights
commit suicide by power surge,
flameless candles devour D batteries,
leave her with unreliable illumination
or in total darkness.

Her tired body betrays:
osteoporotic hips ache,
finger joints freeze,
cervix and vagina shrivel
like dehydrated flowers.

"Ah, my golden years!" she intones,
imbibes liquid THC
with a chaser of Tylenol,
two Melatonin,
a Lexapro nightcap.

Camille's Gratitude List

She gives thanks
for free-spirited,
mature, lusty men.
Takes joy in
a functioning pleasure zone,
testament to effective,
if expensive, estrogen cream.
Compliments her own
tiny nipples,
still-perky breasts.
Praises power walks
along the Pacific
that keep her ass
toned and undimpled.
Counts herself fortunate
to still possess
a supple mind,
wry sense of humor,
all her organs and teeth.

Camille at the Medicare Workshop

As the consultant
draws on his flip chart
and blathers on
about drug plans,
deductibles,
Camille practices
five sets of kegels.
Craves margaritas
or martinis,
maybe a nooner.
Wishes her damp panties
were a reaction to arousal
rather than laughter.
Observes saggy old women,
pot-bellied men
in the chair rows around her.
Wonders why 65 juicy years
have ambushed her patience,
tautness, libido.
Blows off this workshop.
Sneaks out the back door.
Fires up a big doobie.

Camille Mobilizes

*"I'm willing to throw my body
in front of the bus to stop bad ideas."*
—*Elizabeth Warren*

This Place Has Found Us

Camille watches The Donald
cozying up to Sarah Palin,
degenerating MILF,
maverick moron,
Tea Party darling.

It's amazing that so much
willful disinformation
in a confined space
doesn't implode the skulls
of cheering fans
who gather around them.

Camille craves tokes
to erase coming months
of campaign chatter,
political pandering.

Regrets going dry
at a time when
she desperately needs
a prolonged bender,
then sustained blackout.

Raging Grannies

Camille constructs her picket sign,
demands an immediate end to the war on women,
deplores craven male politicians who legislate
against Planned Parenthood,
access to contraception, affordable housing.
She is fed up with guys who discriminate,
call themselves compassionate-conservative Christians.
They fund black ops, promote militarism,
destroy watersheds, rape forests.
Camille has had it with the status quo,
calls out corrupt public figures,
takes her cause to the streets,
stops traffic as she shouts,
"Get your rosaries off our ovaries!"
Supports the sisterhood,
hangs with radical grannies.

Strange Lonely Men

At the grocery store,
Camille discovers lonesome geezers
forlornly pushing shopping carts,
befuddled by produce.
They're unable to tell the difference
between ripe or green,
melon, peach or tomato.

She wonders if this is how
they once chose their women,
grabbing the showiest specimen
from the top of a pyramid
without consideration
for soundness or sweetness.

How many years before
the magic waned
and they strayed,
substituting a younger version
of the same cardboard model?

Squatting Over Their Machines

Camille can't face
one more Zumba,
circuit training or spin class.
Claims her place among treadmills,
stairmasters, rowing machines.
Opts for sixty minutes on a lifecycle,
goaded by the throbbing beat
of Lady Gaga and Bruno Mars.
Joins red-faced, sweaty compadres.
Most listen to music or read magazines
as they struggle and groan.
Others stare at wall-mounted TVs
where flat screens display
carping presidential candidates,
the latest terrorist attacks,
scrolling ticker-tape headlines.
Camille zones out watching "Cupcake Wars,"
pushes her body to burn calories,
trim and tighten problem spots,
delighted by the wicked irony.
Salivates at the construction
of orgasm-inducing,
calorie-laden desserts.

Hot Seat

Camille sits on a squishy sofa
that sends her lower back
into immediate spasm.
Balks at the word "god,"
refuses to recite the serenity prayer
while holding hands with a stranger.

Swallows a lump in her throat
as another woman describes
her alcoholic husband's denial.
Recognizes the sad scenario,
downward spiral.
Decides not to share
her emotions of anger, betrayal.

Agrees with the three C's:
You didn't create it.
Don't control it.
Can't cure it.

Could kick herself in the ass
for not knowing better.

Grass Goes Insane

An armed security guard
at the medical marijuana dispensary
looks Camille over, checks her ID.
He reiterates their cash-only policy,
allows customers into the showroom,
two at a time.

Apothecary jars display
potent buds of dried weed,
imaginative edibles, extracts,
grass in its many incarnations:
sativa, indica, ruderalis.

The shelves are stocked
with assorted oils,
vape cartridges,
pre-rolled joints,
jars of pure THC.

A special nook features
tinctures to ease pain, stimulate appetite,
erase anxiety, treat insomnia.
Others address epilepsy, nausea, PTSD.

Camille chooses from a smorgasbord
of dope delicacies, looks forward
to a weekend sampling
her cannabis treasure trove,
all the ways to get high.

Our Bodies Were Worn

Daily, Camille sees Brody
limping into the gym.
He totters unevenly
from station to station
pumps iron with
his weak arm and leg,
slowly regains strength
after having a stroke.

They nod in passing,
grunt during workouts,
grimace and make noises
that remind her of sex.

His blue eyes follow her progress
at the resistance training machines.
She performs flies, curls, crunches.
He stares at her erect nipples.;
despite tight jogging bra,
they make themselves known.

Camille imagines him naked,
involuntarily moistens.
Visualizes him between her thighs.
Wonders if endorphin overload
and prolonged celibacy
have damaged her brain.

How Did We Get Here?

Camille listens to
potential commanders-in-chief
defile her television screen,
quibbling over the size
of the front-runner's penis.
Argue how rapidly
they would deploy troops,
deny abortion,
deport immigrant workers.
Advocate banning Muslims,
killing off health care.
Boast about embracing
more enhanced torture.
Pledge to target
terrorists' families
for state-sanctioned murder.
Describe vague solutions
to manufactured non-problems.
Pander to bigots.
Reach out to haters.
Brag, ramble and gloat.
Revel in each other's stumbles.
Offer the electorate,
invisible women,
a rickety clown car
of terrible choices.

Better Than Immortality

"Just when you think Donald Trump's opinions
about women and their rights had reached rock bottom, he
managed to quarry even further into some ring of hell that,
until previously, only existed in *Dante's Inferno*."
—Stassa Edwards, The Slot

The Donald declares
he is pro-life,
pronounces abortions
should be banned and
women who have them
must be shamed,
individually *punished.*

It's time for the righteous
to return knocked-up broads
to those *back-alley places*
where they used to go
before a bunch of liberal judges
with no respect for the unborn
gave these sluts a choice,
allowed them to terminate
the fruit of their sins.

He doesn't believe in exceptions
for rape or incest.
Let them reap what they sow.
No consequences for men;
it's not their issue.

Camille grits her teeth,
donates to Planned Parenthood,
sends Elizabeth Warren
a huge contribution.

Lean Back Into It

Camille vapes Sunset Tea marijuana,
watches presidential candidates debate.
She hits the mute button,
improvises moronic non-sequiturs
in the voice of Daffy Duck
on behalf of The Donald.,
invents a pornographic response.

Sick of lies,
mischaracterizations,
political pandering,
she wants to erase
the indelible image
of Trump's white supremacist,
illiterate, misogynistic supporters
as they strut and preen,
spewing virulent hatred
on prime-time TV.

She's had her fill of
impotent moderators,
spin-doctor pundits,
and middle-school squabbles
with lethal implications
for a healthy planet
and any person of conscience.

Ponder Our Imbecilities

Camille is depressed, disillusioned.
Rations news consumption to less
than fifteen minutes a day.
Cannot bear to hear one more
idiotic conspiracy theory.

Has no patience with
screaming shock jocks
inciting violent hate crimes
against lesbians, the transgendered, gays,
women, liberals, people of color.

If she has to watch another
bloated white man over 60
smirk, lie through his teeth,
she'll fling something heavy
through her TV.

Passion Has Its Own Way

Camille has vowed
to give wide berth
to the terminally stupid.
Finds herself unable
to bite her tongue,
listen politely to one more
opinionated moron lacking experience,
knowledge or facts.

She grits her teeth
overhearing remarks
spewed by the arrogantly clueless—
especially those whose decisions
negatively impact her safety,
sanity, self-respect,
financial resources.

Camille loses sleep
as women's rights
are continuously
overturned or eroded.
Vows to seek out
equally infuriated sisters,
focus what energy
she has left to organize, mobilize,
shut down the machine.

The Emperor Has No Clothes

Putin's puppet demands adulation,
military hardware as inauguration accessories,
redecorates the White House
to include golden curtains.

In this post-factual era,
fake news reigns,
black becomes white,
deception the norm,
science and statistics supplanted
by self-serving fictions.

He insists we live in terror,
accept incremental repression,
normalize dismantlement of democracy,
approve attacks on political scapegoats.

Camille and millions of women around the world disagree,
demonstrate, refuse to recognize
an illegitimately installed groper-in-chief,
reject his exaggerations and falsehoods.

Resistance breaks the spell,
reveals naked truth:
the emperor has no clothes;
there is power in numbers.

Tastes Bitter

The newly anointed orange airbag
surrounds himself with authoritarian white men,
signs draconian orders—
issues a global gag rule,
completely rolls back environmental protections,
disconnects the public comments switchboard,
scrubs the White House website.

On Day Two,
he claims millions voted illegally,.
He short-lists potential Supreme Court justices,
rabid conservatives favoring curtailment
of First Amendment rights, civil liberties,
unreasonable searches and seizures.
He green-lights controversial pipelines,
bans federal agencies from social media,
insists on a total news blackout.

California's governor calls out
Trump's universe of non-facts.
Constitutional experts document
President Pussy Grabber's violation
of the emoluments clause, file a lawsuit.

Camille vows not to take these assaults lying down,
bombards legislators with volatile phone calls.

The Unfairness of the Game

> "There's a group of guys in a back room somewhere that
> are making decisions."
> —Sen. Claire McCaskill

Thirteen Republican white men
hide behind a locked door as they
craft a bill to control women's bodies.

They operate in a vacuum of facts,
base legislation on lethal ignorance,
disproved urban legends:

*If it's a legitimate rape, the female body
has ways to try to shut that whole thing down.*

*Who needs abortion when victims of sexual assault
can just get "cleaned out" by a rape kit?*

*Women shouldn't terminate pregnancies
resulting from rape because it's what God intended.*

*Abortion is much more serious
than the rape of children by priests.*

Abortion rights caused the Sandy Hook massacre.

Abortion is just like the Holocaust.

If babies had guns, they wouldn't be aborted.

*Rape is okay when the victim seems
"older than her chronological age."*

*Getting an abortion after being raped
is criminal evidence tampering.*

Senators refuse to share a draft
for review or public comment.
"We aren't stupid," says a GOP aide.

Camille and women with prior experience,
with so much to lose, have a different opinion.

Forget It

Camille fumes while Pussy-Grabber-in-Chief
floods cyberspace
with insane Tourette tweets.
Spineless legislators help
deconstruct federal government,
pander to neo-Nazis, conspiracy nuts.

Critical thinking and civility
succumb within the gas chambers
of faux Fox news
under leadership
of smug white male harassers
bankrolled by rich bottom-feeders.

Forget an era of tolerance,
diversity, social justice.
Rabid reactionaries have
staged a successful coup.
Camille knows the American Dream
is officially over.

Intolerable Conditions

"The right thing to do is pray in moments like this."
—Paul Ryan

Camille reads moronic responses
to the latest assault weapon slaughter,
implores the goddess
to intercede, impose sanity,
vaporize clueless males.

She is fed up with
Second Amendment fanatics
who fail to comprehend that automatic guns
capable of mowing down hundreds
had not been invented
when the constitution was written.

Camille fantasizes a sea of white,
Republican men on their knees,
begging to be spared as she smiles,
presses the trigger of her AK-47,
targets hypocrisy, drops them like flies.

The Night the Muse Dumped You

Camille has nothing;
imagination's needle on empty,
she reads, revises, discards.
Pounds flaccid keyboard.
Prays for a miracle.

She has exceeded her
creative shelf life.
Now it's nothing but rejects
from English majors
enrolled in Literary Magazine 2
to fluff their own vitae.

Didn't I warn you?
sneers a sadistic inner Nazi
who taunts by revealing
the virginal page
she will never deflower.

Her dominatrix muse
bends Camille over the desk,
uncoils a dark whip,
slashes the red ink pen,
makes her aching soul suffer.

Waiting on Death

Camille has no intention
of going out with a whimper.
She'll burn her candle
at both ends,
create maximum uproar.

She imagines gleefully
working her way
down a bucket list
of rude, crude and lewd,
breaking rules with abandon.

Signs up for a nudist weekend,
erotic belly dancing lessons,
an afternoon of sky diving;
restyles her hair to include
lavender highlights.

She sips signature pinot noir
at her favorite bistro, trolls
for an adventuresome playmate
who can appreciate, share
her outrageous intentions.

Camille Comes Unglued

∾

"The truth will set you free, but first it will piss you off."
—*Gloria Steinem*

Tiny Agonies

Camille sips hot coffee,
scrolls through Internet headlines:
Porn Star Says Trump Bad in Bed;
Nuclear War, Extreme Weather
Top List of 2018 Threats;
Marathon Running Mom, 10-Year-Old
Boy Latest Flu Victims;
China space station packed with
'CANCEROUS chemicals'
to crash into Earth 'within MONTHS'.

She is fed up starting every morning
with elevated blood pressure, wanting
to vaporize Washington DC,
exterminate White House residents,
migrate to a remote forest
or desert island
to escape rampant stupidity.
There aren't enough bong hits
to erase oppressive, offensive reality.

Instead, she drags out magic marker,
a huge sheet of poster board
and creates a protest sign
with scathing message, pointed graphics.
She'll share her anger and energy
with vibrant, vocal, voting females
at the local Women's March,
Together, they will oust inept,
sexist clowns currently in power,
bring back intelligent, humane behavior,
take over all levels of government,
make the world sane.

#Time's Up

"One collapses and surrenders…"
—Charles Bukowski

Camille looks forward to the R. Kellys
and Harvey Weinsteins,
predators who can't keep it in their pants,
being apprehended, convicted, jailed.
Encountering their own rapists.

Count her among millions of women
no longer willing to shut the fuck up
about molestation, degradation,
denied career advancement
for another's sick pleasure.

Watch her harness
every iota of energy
to help bring down sexist abusers,
facilitate the dismantling
of patriarchal, enabling culture.

#Time's Up, assholes, she thinks.
Welcome to a brave new world
where women make and enforce rules
to ensure a level playing field,
gender-blind social justice.

Everywhere

"I can't get no satisfaction…"
—Rolling Stones

Camille starts her day at Starbucks
where the body-pierced, tattooed barista
is unable to correctly fill her simple order
for a latte, flubs counting change.

Later, she navigates the crowded freeway.
Drivers wildly change lanes without
using their signals; slow cars obstruct traffic.
Cal-trans blocks the exit she needs.

Swerving to avoid a moron,
she watches as $5.00 of designer coffee
splashes into her lap, onto the seat where
it stains beige sweater, gray upholstery.

At her support group meeting,
Camille recites the opening preamble,
seethes, shares an inventory of grievances,
is anything but serene.

Meltdown

"What is there to say about former Mayor of New York City
Rudy Giuliani that hasn't been farted into a bag and fed to
a demon for punishment?"
—*Daily Kos*

Camille reads Rudy's latest mental meanderings
in response to Pussy-Grabber-in-Chief's
senile behavior, tone-deaf remarks.
The phrase "Takes one to know one"
sticks in her mind.

Co-conspiring, seditious white men
discover privilege is not permanent.
As Mueller's investigation documents
layers of perjured malfeasance,
potential indictments gnaw at their heels.

Giuliani's dementia escalates,
manifests itself in social media postings
as he incriminates his oblivious client and self.
The shit show unravels before Camille's eyes,
pervasive treason revealed.

Her Golden Years

Now that Camille is pushing 70,
solicitation phone calls are never-ending.
Her mailbox overflows with ads
for cremation, hearing aids,
assisted living.

Doctors refuse to listen
to descriptions of symptoms.
They attribute aches and pains
to advancing age,
rarely bother to order
diagnostic blood tests or x-rays.

Increasingly fragile, Camille
no longer jogs or pumps iron,
swallows handfuls of supplements,
might dislocate or break bones
with the simple act
of just bending over.

Crazy

Camille notices a woman in the pharmacy
checkout line as she unloads her basket:
home pregnancy test, bag of Doritos,
midnight blue eyeliner,
toy Jedi light saber.

The gal's torn Metallica tee shirt
clings by a thread,
has seen better days.
She flaunts chipped ebony toenails,
wears faded Levi's.

A drunk, homeless man hits Camille up
for a dollar as she walks to her car.
She contemplates the unraveling social asylum,
everyone looking for whatever erases or numbs,
doing what they can to get by.

Not Worth It

Camille hasn't
the patience for
more
complications,
decides to
swear off
abrasive
meetings,
earnest
pollsters,
high-maintenance relatives.

In this culture of cruelty,
she chooses not to participate
in the ongoing
Stanford
experiment
of power and
corruption,
concentrates on
creation,
entertains
spoiled dogs.

She
surrounds
herself
with Big Sur
beauty,
blooming
Columbine,
nourishing
friends.

Goddess-zilla Gets Woke

"You look prettier when you smile!"
strangers shout at Camille as they pass.
At professional meetings,
her supervisor reprimands
when she objects to interruptions,
says she sounds shrill.

A creepy ex-partner
emails out of the blue,
asks for her telephone number
so he can reconnect, share details
about his adventuresome life.
She deletes his message,
makes sure he is blocked.

Rage bubbles inside her
from a lifetime of indoctrination,
demands she remain invisible, acquiescent.
Fury fuels her awakening,
a decision to break glass ceilings,
overthrow repressive conditioning,
achieve radical change.

Grabbing her pussy hat
and picket sign,
she joins her sisters
as they march,
link arms and chant,
confront their oppressors,
take back the streets.

Something That Will Help

"...just a shot away..."
—Rolling Stones

Camille discovers cannabis tincture
at the local dispensary,
credits this magic potion
for altering perspective,
lifting her spirits.

THC erases current events,
eases anxiety,
mollifies anger.

At night, a dropper or two
insures unbroken sleep,
restful dreams,
a chemical amnesia
to survive until morning.

The Dead-before-death Gang

They wear geezerdom
like scruffy badges of honor,
snarl at women who enter their lair—
a fetid saloon for cranky,
resentful men who have succumbed
to stale testosterone poisoning.

Looking in, Camille sees a gang
of the living dead.
They drive away all who care
with their pissing and moaning,
communally nurse escalating
bitterness, grudges.

They fester and stew,
obsess over ancient, exaggerated wrongs,
take privilege for granted,
imagine vindictive revenge.
The 21st Century
passes them by.

Turned and Walked Away

"I truly loved you, put no one above you.
Now I'm walking away."
—Jonny Lang

Camille's fire has burned itself out.
Lovers who once left her aching
now fail to satisfy, just piss her off.

In her thirties, she moistened
as she imagined sexual conquests
and erotic, fantasy fucks.

Now her hip joints ache.
Exhaustion overwhelms by 9 p.m.
Age makes her its unwilling bitch.

Romance seems too much work.
All she wants is peace and quiet,
a quaint little cottage with stabilized rent.

You Grow Transformed

Camille hasn't felt cold
since she turned 55.
When silver foxes approach,
latent estrogen flares,
briefly lights her up like a torch.

In bed, however,
intimate body parts no longer
fit together smoothly
or bring sensual pleasure
as in the past.

There's little on the market
to erase hard years,
rejuvenate what invisibly pinches,
spasms and sags.

Camille's fickle flesh
is uncooperative,
thwarts desire,
has closed up shop,
gone out on strike.

Camille Comes Unglued

> "It's a complex issue because one has to think,
> well there's a host body and that host body has to have
> a certain amount of rights because at the end of the day
> it is that body that that carries this entire other body
> to term. But there is an additional life there."
> —Newly Elected Florida House Speaker José Oliva

Camille reads the quote, becomes incandescent.
Despises arrogant misogyny, an ignorant belief that
she's nothing more than a baby container.
Vows to support progressive women candidates
so every female can control her own body.

She wonders how men would react
if redesignated as insentient hosts,
each drop of semen conferred with
personhood rights that outweighed
male intentions and interests.

If it impacted them, would obtuse dudes
oppose governmental interference,
unqualified legislators in the driver's seat
making decisions regarding
another's reproductive organs?

Camille listens to a procession
of smug, self-righteous old guys
pontificate on the sanctity of the pre-born,
discovers she is fresh out of fucks to give,
grows increasingly livid with rage.

Sleep Alone

Camille has replaced lovers
with two snugly dogs,
an extra-large pillow.
Finds she prefers
sprawling comfortably alone
in her own king-size bed.

At night, she can stretch,
snore if she wishes.
Let erotic dreams bloom.
Slip one foot out
from under the quilt
without male obstruction.

Camille Hits the Wall

It's week ten of sheltering in place.
Camille's stylish hairdo has devolved
into a silver tangle of cowlicks, split ends.
Her scarlet fingers and toes revert
to hangnails, ragged cuticles.
Thick calluses reclaim the soles of her feet.
The novelty of free time has worn off.
She is sick of reruns, has cleaned and organized
every cupboard and closet, dead-headed flowers,
scoured the garden of weeds.

Once obsessed over stylish couture, dangly earrings,
now she worries about having an adequate supply
of toilet paper, Nitrile gloves, an assortment of masks.
Grocery shopping is conducted online with DoorDash delivery
or after suiting up in protective gear as if walking in space.
Security guards monitor the store entrance.
One-way aisles are labeled with arrows and signs,
warn shoppers to remain at least six feet apart.
Checkout lines lengthen as clerks behind Plexiglas shields
sanitize counters and credit card keypad between customers.
Back home, she wipes down each purchase,
strips to shower, washes what she's worn.

Each day, when walls close in upon her,
confinement chafes, irritability blossoms.
She reminds herself how lucky she is
to still have income, health, a helpful partner,
large yard and spacious home with tons of books,
a writing room for herself.

Absolution

"Where the sea recedes..."
—Joan Colby

King tides sluice ashore, erase footprints,
bury broken seashells, repossess clots of flotsam.
Tabula rasa sands cradle twitching blue ocean.

Lupine, orange poppies camouflage forest burn scars.
Forking deer trails traverse ridge tops,
challenge temptation to explore new directions.

After a year of isolation, Camille embraces her inner hermit,
discovers a growing inability to reconnect,
an unwillingness to resume a destructive old normal.

Needled cactus passively fend off intruders.
She prefers a locked door, empty calendar squares,
lone meanders through redwoods.

White-cowled lilies cluster in shadow.
Solitary confinement restores frazzled nerves.
Serenity bathes Camille's ragged soul, confers absolution.

Genesis Extravaganza

Camille squeezes into her orchestra seat
at San Francisco's Regency Ballroom.
It's exactly the sausage fest she expected:
at least six bald, slogan-tee-shirted men
for every outnumbered woman.

Around her, beer-guzzling early Genesis buffs,
a sea of enlarged prostates, involuntary celibates,
potential erectile dysfunction.
She comforts herself with the thought
there won't be uncomfortable lines
at too few women's restrooms.

On stage, five French Canadian musicians
with long, swinging hair
wearing white yoga pants perform
framed by a slide show of obscure artwork.
She can't recognize a single song.

Bizarre costumes, interminable drum riffs,
flailing arms, clouds of cannabis vapors
envelope the sardine-packed audience.
Camille yawns, prepares to exit
as a balcony filled with LSD-tripping
retreads from the seventies sing along
with the band, dance their hearts out.

Crone Collaborative

Camille's cronies call each other goddesses,
dress in vintage thrift-shop gowns,
wear sparkling plastic tiaras,
are subjects of envious gossip among the senior set,
hang out at bohemian bars
in the wilds of Big Sur.

They have each other's back,
listen without judgment,
commiserate during breakups,
hookups, illness, infirmity,
financial hardship,
family deaths.

They exchange house keys,
security codes,
Internet passwords.
Share names of therapists,
publishing contacts,
massage technicians.

Vowing to start
their own geriatric commune,
they can't imagine life
without this supportive sisterhood
of sympathetic soulmates,
irreverent friends.

Dirty Fingernails

"Gardening is an instrument of grace."
—May Sarton

Camille seeks sunlight, hauls poetry into spring garden,
settles among bearded iris, cascading alyssum,
scribbles in her journal, reads a new book.

Swallows discover a white hair strand,
carry the orphan ringlet under roof eave,
weave a piece of her into their nest.

A boorish jay perches on a power line,
bobs and croaks, showing off for his mate.
Camille deadheads spent geraniums, plucks dandelions.

All in all, it's a productive afternoon: solar vitamin D,
a rough draft of new verse, only one broken fingernail,
soul soothed by industry, smudge of dirt on her face.

Rebirth

"The birds still remember
what we have forgotten..."
—Terry Tempest Williams

If she could choose reincarnation,
Camille would return to earth as a blue jay,
bird equivalent of a crude uncle
who pinches women as they pass,
quotes Tucker Carlson,
farts at the table.
What a relief it would be to shed
delicate hummingbird manners,
bluster until she gets her way,
greedily gorge on every seed in the feeder,
sharpen her beak
against garden sculptures.
Camille would unleash her inner pterodactyl,
revel in self-entitlement,
take whatever she wants
when she wants,
intimidate sparrows and finches,
make frightened wrens scatter.

Acknowledgments

The author is grateful for the editorial assistance provided by Diane Kistner, Joan Colby, Charles Rammelkamp, Kate Aver Avraham, Laura Bayless and Gene McCormick.

Some of these poems have appeared in the following publications, sometimes in a slightly different form.

Abbey: "Sadly Sane"
Dead Snakes: "Expatriate," "Carne," "Mimo," "Madrid," "Beach Esplanade," "Tapas y Tequila," "This Place Has Found Us"
I Am Not a Silent Poet: "Tiny Agonies"
In Between Hangovers: "Everywhere"
misfitmagazine.net: "Alicante," "Emigrada," "Rainstorm"
Pif Magazine: "Dirty Fingernails"
The Potomac: "Same Old Movie," "So Much Has Gone," "Camille at the Medicare Workshop"
Silver Birch Press, My Mane Memories Theme: "Mane Events"
SNReview: "Peaches and Camille, Post Pinot Noir"
Trajectory: "Kryptonite"
Wilderness House Literary Review: "Art of the Wild," "Camille at the Creekside Café," "Camille Behind the Wheel"
Winedrunk Sidewalk: "Meltdown," "Crazy," "Goddess-zilla Gets Woke," "Dead-before-death Gang"
Your One Phone Call: "Shot to Hell"

About FutureCycle Press

FutureCycle Press is dedicated to publishing lasting English-language poetry in both print-on-demand and Kindle formats. Founded in 2007 by long-time independent editor/publishers and partners Diane Kistner and Robert S. King, the press was incorporated as a nonprofit in 2012. A number of our editors are distinguished poets and writers in their own right, and we have been actively involved in the small press movement going back to the early seventies.

Each year, we award the FutureCycle Poetry Book Prize and honorarium for the best original full-length volume of poetry we published that year. Introduced in 2013, proceeds from our Good Works projects are donated to charity. Our Selected Poems series highlights contemporary poets with a substantial body of work to their credit; with this series we strive to resurrect work that has had limited distribution and is now out of print.

We are dedicated to giving all of the authors we publish the care their work deserves, offering a catalog of the most diverse and distinguished work possible, and paying forward any earnings to fund more great books. All of our books are kept "alive" and available unless and until an author requests a title be taken out of print.

We've learned a few things about independent publishing over the years. We've also evolved a unique and resilient publishing model that allows us to focus mainly on vetting and preserving for posterity poetry collections of exceptional quality without becoming overwhelmed with bookkeeping and mailing, fundraising activities, or taxing editorial and production "bubbles." To find out more about what we are doing, come see us at www.futurecycle.org.

www.ingramcontent.com/pod-product-compliance
Lightning Source LLC
Chambersburg PA
CBHW072358090426
42741CB00012B/3076